TRUMPET

The BIG BOOK of
trumpet songs

AVAILABLE FOR:
Flute, Clarinet, Alto Sax, Tenor Sax, Trumpet,
Horn, Trombone, Violin, Viola, and Cello

ISBN 978-1-4234-2667-7

Visit Hal Leonard Online at
www.halleonard.com

Contact Us:
Hal Leonard
7777 West Bluemound Road
Milwaukee, WI 53213
Email: info@halleonard.com

In Europe contact:
Hal Leonard Europe Limited
Distribution Centre, Newmarket Road
Bury St Edmunds, Suffolk, IP33 3YB
Email: info@halleonardeurope.com

In Australia contact:
Hal Leonard Australia Pty. Ltd.
4 Lentara Court
Cheltenham, Victoria, 3192 Australia
Email: info@halleonard.com.au

CONTENTS

ALL MY LOVING

from A HARD DAY'S NIGHT

TRUMPET

Words and Music by JOHN LENNON
and PAUL McCARTNEY

ALL THE SMALL THINGS

TRUMPET

Words and Music by TOM DE LONGE
and MARK HOPPUS

Bright driving Rock

ALLEY CAT

TRUMPET

By FRANK BJORN

Moderately slow

ANOTHER ONE BITES THE DUST

TRUMPET

Words and Music by
JOHN DEACON

Steady Rock

To Coda ⊕   1.

2.

D.C. al Coda

CODA ⊕

AMERICA

from the Motion Picture THE JAZZ SINGER

TRUMPET

Words and Music by
NEIL DIAMOND

Moderately

ANY DREAM WILL DO

from JOSEPH AND THE AMAZING TECHNICOLOR® DREAMCOAT

TRUMPET

Music by ANDREW LLOYD WEBBER
Lyrics by TIM RICE

BE TRUE TO YOUR SCHOOL

TRUMPET

Words and Music by BRIAN WILSON
and MIKE LOVE

Slowly

BAD DAY

TRUMPET

Words and Music by
DANIEL POWTER

D.S. al Coda

CODA

BARELY BREATHING

TRUMPET

Words and Music by
DUNCAN SHEIK

(It's A)
BEAUTIFUL MORNING

TRUMPET

Words and Music by FELIX CAVALIERE
and EDWARD BRIGATI, JR.

BEAUTY AND THE BEAST
from Walt Disney's BEAUTY AND THE BEAST

TRUMPET

Lyrics by HOWARD ASHMAN
Music by ALAN MENKEN

Moderately slow

BEYOND THE SEA

TRUMPET

Words and Music by CHARLES TRENET,
ALBERT LASRY and JACK LAWRENCE

BLACKBIRD

TRUMPET

Words and Music by JOHN LENNON
and PAUL McCARTNEY

BLUE SUEDE SHOES

TRUMPET

Words and Music by
CARL LEE PERKINS

BOOGIE WOOGIE BUGLE BOY

from BUCK PRIVATES

TRUMPET

Words and Music by DON RAYE
and HUGHIE PRINCE

THE BRADY BUNCH
Theme from the Paramount Television Series THE BRADY BUNCH

TRUMPET

Words and Music by SHERWOOD SCHWARTZ
and FRANK DEVOL

BUTTERFLY KISSES

TRUMPET

Words and Music by BOB CARLISLE
and RANDY THOMAS

BREAKING FREE

from the Disney Channel Original Movie HIGH SCHOOL MUSICAL

TRUMPET

Words and Music by
JAMIE HOUSTON

Moderately

CABARET
from the Musical CABARET

Words by FRED EBB
Music by JOHN KANDER

TRUMPET

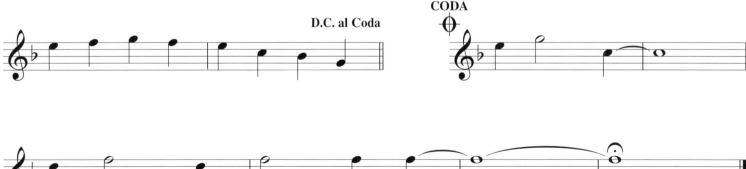

CALIFORNIA DREAMIN'

TRUMPET

Words and Music by JOHN PHILLIPS
and MICHELLE PHILLIPS

CANDLE IN THE WIND

TRUMPET

Words and Music by ELTON JOHN
and BERNIE TAUPIN

CHIM CHIM CHER-EE

from Walt Disney's MARY POPPINS

TRUMPET

Words and Music by RICHARD M. SHERMAN
and ROBERT B. SHERMAN

CLOCKS

TRUMPET

Words and Music by GUY BERRYMAN, JON BUCKLAND,
WILL CHAMPION and CHRIS MARTIN

(They Long to Be)

CLOSE TO YOU

TRUMPET

Lyric by HAL DAVID
Music by BURT BACHARACH

COLORS OF THE WIND
from Walt Disney's POCAHONTAS

TRUMPET

Music by ALAN MENKEN
Lyrics by STEPHEN SCHWARTZ

COME FLY WITH ME

TRUMPET

Words by SAMMY CAHN
Music by JAMES VAN HEUSEN

COPACABANA
(At the Copa)
from Barry Manilow's COPACABANA

TRUMPET

Music by BARRY MANILOW
Lyric by BRUCE SUSSMAN and JACK FELDMAN

Moderately, with a Latin feel

DO-RE-MI
from THE SOUND OF MUSIC

TRUMPET

Lyrics by OSCAR HAMMERSTEIN II
Music by RICHARD RODGERS

DO WAH DIDDY DIDDY

TRUMPET

Words and Music by JEFF BARRY
and ELLIE GREENWICH

(Sittin' On)
THE DOCK OF THE BAY

TRUMPET

Words and Music by STEVE CROPPER
and OTIS REDDING

DON'T BE CRUEL
(To a Heart That's True)

TRUMPET

Words and Music by OTIS BLACKWELL
and ELVIS PRESLEY

DON'T LET THE SUN GO DOWN ON ME

TRUMPET

Words and Music by ELTON JOHN
and BERNIE TAUPIN

Slow Rock

DON'T SPEAK

TRUMPET

Words and Music by ERIC STEFANI
and GWEN STEFANI

D.S. al Coda

CODA

small notes optional

DRIFT AWAY

TRUMPET

Words and Music by
MENTOR WILLIAMS

Moderately fast

To Coda ⊕

D.C. al Coda

CODA ⊕

DUKE OF EARL

TRUMPET

Words and Music by EARL EDWARDS,
EUGENE DIXON and BERNICE WILLIAMS

THEME FROM E.T. (THE EXTRA-TERRESTRIAL)

from the Universal Picture E.T. (THE EXTRA-TERRESTRIAL)

TRUMPET

Music by
JOHN WILLIAMS

EDELWEISS
from THE SOUND OF MUSIC

TRUMPET

Lyrics by OSCAR HAMMERSTEIN II
Music by RICHARD RODGERS

EVERY BREATH YOU TAKE

TRUMPET

Music and Lyrics by
STING

EVERYTHING IS BEAUTIFUL

TRUMPET

Words and Music by
RAY STEVENS

Moderately fast

FALLIN'

TRUMPET

Words and Music by
ALICIA KEYS

Freely **Medium Blues**

FIELDS OF GOLD

TRUMPET

Music and Lyrics by
STING

FLY LIKE AN EAGLE

TRUMPET

Words and Music by
STEVE MILLER

FOR ONCE IN MY LIFE

TRUMPET

Words by RONALD MILLER
Music by ORLANDO MURDEN

FOREVER YOUNG

TRUMPET

Words and Music by ROD STEWART,
JIM CREGAN, KEVIN SAVIGAR and BOB DYLAN

Driving beat

FUN, FUN, FUN

TRUMPET

Words and Music by BRIAN WILSON
and MIKE LOVE

Bright Rock

THE GIRL FROM IPANEMA
(Garôta de Ipanema)

TRUMPET

Music by ANTONIO CARLOS JOBIM
English Words by NORMAN GIMBEL
Original Words by VINICIUS DE MORAES

Bossa Nova

GOD BLESS THE U.S.A

TRUMPET

Words and Music by
LEE GREENWOOD

GONNA BUILD A MOUNTAIN

from the Musical Production STOP THE WORLD – I WANT TO GET OFF

TRUMPET

Words and Music by LESLIE BRICUSSE
and ANTHONY NEWLEY

Moderately bright

GOODBYE YELLOW BRICK ROAD

TRUMPET

Words and Music by ELTON JOHN
and BERNIE TAUPIN

Moderately slow, in 2

GREEN GREEN GRASS OF HOME

TRUMPET

Words and Music by
CURLY PUTMAN

Slowly

HAPPY DAYS

Theme from the Paramount Television Series HAPPY DAYS

TRUMPET

Words by NORMAN GIMBEL
Music by CHARLES FOX

HAVE I TOLD YOU LATELY

TRUMPET

Words and Music by
VAN MORRISON

HEART AND SOUL

from the Paramount Short Subject A SONG IS BORN

Words by FRANK LOESSER
Music by HOAGY CARMICHAEL

TRUMPET

Moderately, lightly rhythmical

HOGAN'S HEROES MARCH
from the Television Series HOGAN'S HEROES

TRUMPET

By JERRY FIELDING

HERE WITHOUT YOU

TRUMPET

Words and Music by MATT ROBERTS,
BRAD ARNOLD, CHRISTOPHER HENDERSON
and ROBERT HARRELL

Moderate Rock

I DREAMED A DREAM
from LES MISÉRABLES

TRUMPET

Music by CLAUDE-MICHEL SCHÖNBERG
Lyrics by ALAIN BOUBLIL, JEAN-MARC NATEL
and HERBERT KRETZMER

I HEARD IT THROUGH THE GRAPEVINE

TRUMPET

Words and Music by NORMAN J. WHITFIELD
and BARRETT STRONG

I SAY A LITTLE PRAYER

TRUMPET

Lyric by HAL DAVID
Music by BURT BACHARACH

Moderately fast

I WHISTLE A HAPPY TUNE

from THE KING AND I

TRUMPET

Lyrics by OSCAR HAMMERSTEIN II
Music by RICHARD RODGERS

Brightly

I WILL REMEMBER YOU
Theme from THE BROTHERS McMULLEN

TRUMPET

Words and Music by SARAH McLACHLAN,
SEAMUS EGAN and DAVE MERENDA

I WRITE THE SONGS

TRUMPET

Words and Music by
BRUCE JOHNSTON

Slow Ballad

I'M POPEYE THE SAILOR MAN

Theme from the Paramount Cartoon POPEYE THE SAILOR

Words and Music by
SAMMY LERNER

TRUMPET

Moderately

IF I EVER LOSE MY FAITH IN YOU

TRUMPET

Music and Lyrics by
STING

IMAGINE

TRUMPET

Words and Music by
JOHN LENNON

Medium slow

IT'S MY LIFE

TRUMPET

Words and Music by JON BON JOVI,
RICHARD SAMBORA and MARTIN SANDBERG

IT'S STILL ROCK AND ROLL TO ME

TRUMPET

Words and Music by
BILLY JOEL

JAILHOUSE ROCK

TRUPMET

Words and Music by JERRY LEIBER
and MIKE STOLLER

JOY TO THE WORLD

TRUMPET

Words and Music by
HOYT AXTON

JUMP, JIVE AN' WAIL

TRUMPET

Words and Music by
LOUIS PRIMA

KANSAS CITY

TRUMPET

Words and Music by JERRY LEIBER
and MIKE STOLLER

KOKOMO
from the Motion Picture COCKTAIL

TRUMPET

Words and Music by MIKE LOVE, TERRY MELCHER,
JOHN PHILLIPS and SCOTT McKENZIE

Moderately bright

LET 'EM IN

TRUMPET

Words and Music by
PAUL and LINDA McCARTNEY

LET'S STAY TOGETHER

TRUMPET

Words and Music by AL GREEN,
WILLIE MITCHELL and AL JACKSON, JR.

LIKE A ROCK

TRUMPET

Words and Music by
BOB SEGER

LIVIN' LA VIDA LOCA

TRUMPET

Words and Music by ROBI ROSA
and DESMOND CHILD

Fast, with a steady beat

LOVE AND MARRIAGE

TRUMPET

Words by SAMMY CAHN
Music by JAMES VAN HEUSEN

LOVE STORY
Theme from the Paramount Picture LOVE STORY

TRUMPET

Music by FRANCIS LAI

MAGGIE MAY

TRUMPET

Words and Music by ROD STEWART
and MARTIN QUITTENTON

Moderately bright

MAKING OUR DREAMS COME TRUE

Theme from the Paramount Television Series LAVERNE AND SHIRLEY

Words by NORMAN GIMBEL
Music by CHARLES FOX

TRUMPET

Bright 4

MAYBE I'M AMAZED

TRUMPET

Words and Music by
PAUL McCARTNEY

MICHELLE

TRUMPET

Words and Music by JOHN LENNON
and PAUL McCARTNEY

MICKEY MOUSE MARCH

from Walt Disney's THE MICKEY MOUSE CLUB

TRUMPET

Words and Music by
JIMMIE DODD

MISSION: IMPOSSIBLE THEME

From the Paramount Television Series MISSION: IMPOSSIBLE

TRUMPET

By LALO SCHIFRIN

Moderately, with drive

MISTER SANDMAN

TRUMPET

Lyric and Music by
PAT BALLARD

MOON RIVER

from the Paramount Picture BREAKFAST AT TIFFANY'S

TRUMPET

Words by JOHNNY MERCER
Music by HENRY MANCINI

Slowly

MY HEART WILL GO ON
(Love Theme from 'Titanic')
from the Paramount and Twentieth Century Fox Motion Picture TITANIC

TRUMPET

Music by JAMES HORNER
Lyric by WILL JENNINGS

Moderately

small notes optional

MY WAY

TRUMPET

English Words by PAUL ANKA
Original French Words by GILLES THIBAULT
Music by JACQUES REVAUX and CLAUDE FRANCOIS

NA NA HEY HEY KISS HIM GOODBYE

TRUMPET

Words and Music by ARTHUR FRASHUER DALE,
PAUL ROGER LEKA and GARY CARLA

ON BROADWAY

TRUMPET

Words and Music by BARRY MANN,
CYNTHIA WEIL, MIKE STOLLER and JERRY LEIBER

PEPPERMINT TWIST

TRUPET

Words and Music by JOSEPH DiNICOLA
and HENRY GLOVER

POCKETFUL OF MIRACLES

TRUMPET

Words by SAMMY CAHN
Music by JAMES VAN HEUSEN

Moderately, with a lilt

PUFF THE MAGIC DRAGON

TRUMPET

Words and Music by LENNY LIPTON
and PETER YARROW

PUT YOUR HAND IN THE HAND

TRUMPET

Words and Music by
GENE MacLELLAN

QUIET NIGHTS OF QUIET STARS
(Corcovado)

TRUMPET

English Words by GENE LEES
Original Words and Music by ANTONIO CARLOS JOBIM

Moderately slow

ROCK AROUND THE CLOCK

TRUPMET

Words and Music by MAX C. FREEDMAN
and JIMMY DeKNIGHT

ROCK WITH YOU

TRUMPET

Words and Music by
ROD TEMPERTON

Moderate Rock

SATIN DOLL

TRUMPET

By DUKE ELLINGTON

SAVE THE BEST FOR LAST

TRUMPET

Words and Music by PHIL GALDSTON,
JON LIND and WENDY WALDMAN

THEME FROM "SCHINDLER'S LIST"

from the Universal Motion Picture SCHINDLER'S LIST

TRUMPET

Music by JOHN WILLIAMS

SHE WILL BE LOVED

TRUMPET

Words and Music by ADAM LEVINE
and JAMES VALENTINE

SING
from SESAME STREET

TRUMPET

Words and Music by
JOE RAPOSO

SO LONG, FAREWELL
from THE SOUND OF MUSIC

TRUMPET

Lyrics by OSCAR HAMMERSTEIN II
Music by RICHARD RODGERS

SOMEWHERE OUT THERE

from AN AMERICAN TAIL

TRUMPET

Music by BARRY MANN and JAMES HORNER
Lyric by CYNTHIA WEIL

SPANISH FLEA

TRUMPET

Words and Music by
JULIUS WECHTER

Moderately

STACY'S MOM

TRUMPET

Words and Music by CHRIS COLLINGWOOD
and ADAM SCHLESINGER

SUNRISE, SUNSET
from the Musical FIDDLER ON THE ROOF

TRUMPET

Words by SHELDON HARNICK
Music by JERRY BOCK

Moderately slow Waltz tempo

TAKE MY BREATH AWAY
(Love Theme)
from the Paramount Picture TOP GUN

Words and Music by GIORGIO MORODER
and TOM WHITLOCK

TRUMPET

THAT'S AMORÉ
(That's Love)
from the Paramount Picture THE CADDY

Words by JACK BROOKS
Music by HARRY WARREN

TRUMPET

THIS LAND IS YOUR LAND

TRUMPET

Words and Music by
WOODY GUTHRIE

THOSE WERE THE DAYS

TRUMPET

Words and Music by
GENE RASKIN

TIME AFTER TIME

TRUMPET

Words and Music by CYNDI LAUPER
and ROB HYMAN

A THOUSAND MILES

TRUMPET

Words and Music by
VANESSA CARLTON

TOMORROW
from the Musical Production ANNIE

TRUMPET

Lyric by MARTIN CHARNIN
Music by CHARLES STROUSE

TOP OF THE WORLD

TRUMPET

Words and Music by JOHN BETTIS
and RICHARD CARPENTER

TWIST AND SHOUT

TRUMPET

Words and Music by BERT RUSSELL
and PHIL MEDLEY

UNCHAINED MELODY

TRUMPET

Lyric by HY ZARET
Music by ALEX NORTH

UNDER THE BOARDWALK

TRUMPET

Words and Music by ARTIE RESNICK
and KENNY YOUNG

UNITED WE STAND

TRUMPET

Words and Music by ANTHONY TOBY HILLER
and JOHN GOODISON

THE WAY YOU MOVE

TRUMPET

Words and Music by ANTWAN PATTON,
PATRICK BROWN and CARLTON MAHONE

WE ARE THE WORLD

TRUMPET

Words and Music by LIONEL RICHIE
and MICHAEL JACKSON

WE BELONG TOGETHER

TRUMPET

Words and Music by MARIAH CAREY,
JERMAINE DUPRI, MANUEL SEAL, JOHNTA AUSTIN,
DARNELL BRISTOL, KENNETH EDMONDS, SIDNEY JOHNSON,
PATRICK MOTEN, BOBBY WOMACK and SANDRA SULLY

Slow Soul

WHAT THE WORLD NEEDS NOW IS LOVE

TRUMPET

Lyric by HAL DAVID
Music by BURT BACHARACH

WITH A LITTLE HELP FROM MY FRIENDS

TRUMPET

Words and Music by JOHN LENNON
and PAUL McCARTNEY

WONDERFUL TONIGHT

TRUMPET

Words and Music by
ERIC CLAPTON

WOOLY BULLY

TRUMPET

Words and Music by
DOMINGO SAMUDIO

Moderately

small notes optional

YELLOW SUBMARINE

TRUMPET

Words and Music by JOHN LENNON
and PAUL McCARTNEY

YOU ARE THE SUNSHINE OF MY LIFE

TRUMPET

Words and Music by
STEVIE WONDER

Moderately

YOU RAISE ME UP

TRUMPET

Words and Music by BRENDAN GRAHAM
and ROLF LOVLAND

YOU'VE GOT A FRIEND

TRUMPET

Words and Music by
CAROLE KING

ZIP-A-DEE-DOO-DAH

from Walt Disney's SONG OF THE SOUTH
from Disneyland and Walt Disney World's SPLASH MOUNTAIN

TRUMPET

Words by RAY GILBERT
Music by ALLIE WRUBEL